ELVIS PRESLEY™

SUPER EASY SONGBOOK

T0086837

ISBN 978-1-70514-631-6

ELVIS™ and ELVIS PRESLEY™ are trademarks of ABG EPE IP LLC
Rights of Publicity and Persona Rights: Elvis Presley Enterprises, LLC
© 2021 ABG EPE IP LLC
elvis.com

Cover photo Getty Images / Sunset Boulevard / Contributor

Contact us:
Hal Leonard
7777 West Bluemound Road
Milwaukee, WI 53213
Email: info@halleonard.com

In Europe, contact:
Hal Leonard Europe Limited
42 Wigmore Street
Marylebone, London, W1U 2RN
Email: info@halleonardeurope.com

In Australia, contact:
Hal Leonard Australia Pty. Ltd.
4 Lentara Court
Cheltenham, Victoria, 3192 Australia
Email: info@halleonard.com.au

Welcome to the *Super Easy Songbook* series!

This unique collection will help you play your favorite songs quickly and easily. Here's how it works:

- Play the simplified melody with your right hand. Letter names appear inside each note to assist you.

- There are no key signatures to worry about! If a sharp ♯ or flat ♭ is needed, it is shown beside the note each time.

- There are no page turns, so your hands never have to leave the keyboard.

- If two notes are connected by a tie ‿, hold the first note for the combined number of beats. (The second note does not show a letter name since it is not re-struck.)

- Add basic chords with your left hand using the provided keyboard diagrams. Chord voicings have been carefully chosen to minimize hand movement.

- The left-hand rhythm is up to you, and chord notes can be played together or separately. Be creative!

- If the chords sound muddy, move your left hand an octave* higher. If this gets in the way of playing the melody, move your right hand an octave higher as well.

  * *An octave spans eight notes. If your starting note is C, the next C to the right is an octave higher.*

———————————————— ALSO AVAILABLE ————————————————

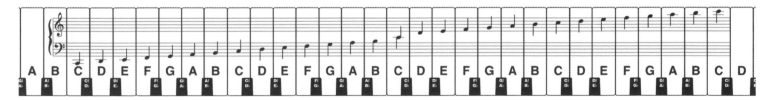

Hal Leonard Student Keyboard Guide HL00296039

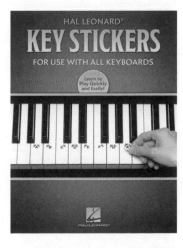

Key Stickers HL00100016

All Shook Up

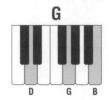
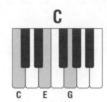
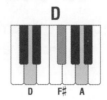

Words and Music by Otis Blackwell
and Elvis Presley

Bright Shuffle

A - well - a, bless my soul; ___ what's wrong with me? I'm
hands are shak - y and my knees are weak. I

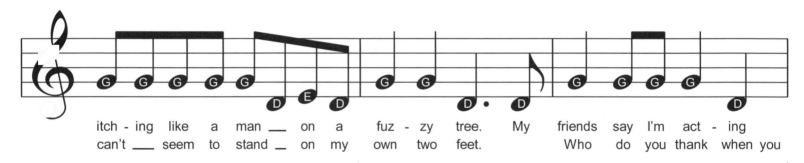

itch - ing like a man ___ on a fuz - zy tree. My friends say I'm act - ing
can't ___ seem to stand ___ on my own two feet. Who do you thank when you

(no chord)
N.C.

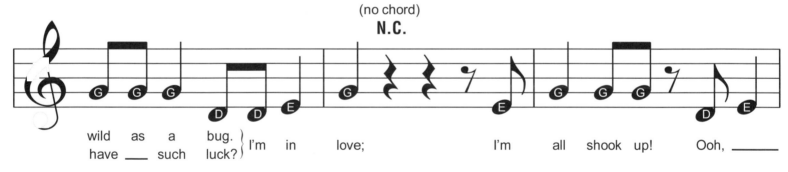

wild as a bug. ⎱
have ___ such luck? ⎰ I'm in love; I'm all shook up! Ooh, ___

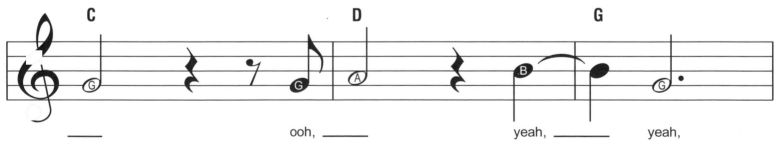

___ ooh, ___ yeah, ___ yeah,

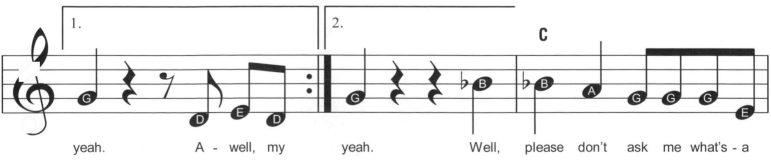

yeah. A - well, my yeah. Well, please don't ask me what's - a

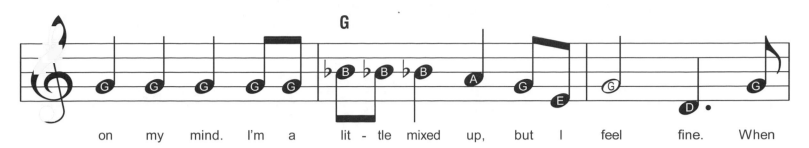

on my mind. I'm a lit-tle mixed up, but I feel fine. When

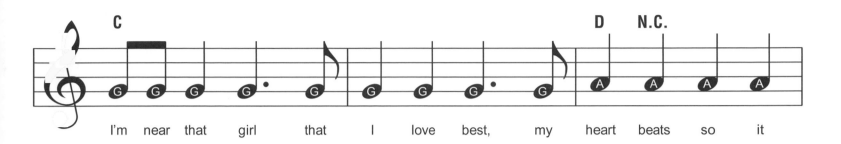

I'm near that girl that I love best, my heart beats so it

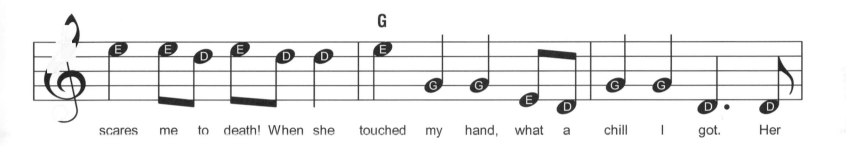

scares me to death! When she touched my hand, what a chill I got. Her

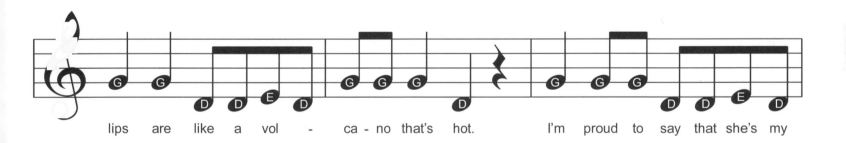

lips are like a vol-ca-no that's hot. I'm proud to say that she's my

but-ter-cup. I'm in _____ love. I'm all shook up! Ooh, _____

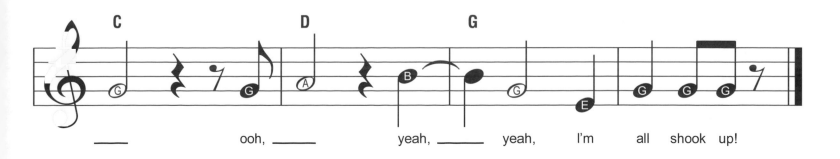

_____ ooh, _____ yeah, _____ yeah, I'm all shook up!

Are You Lonesome Tonight?

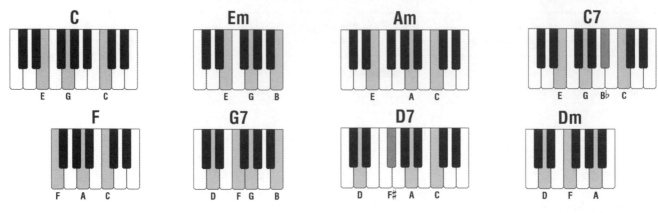

Words and Music by Roy Turk
and Lou Handman

Moderately slow

Are you lone - some to - night? Do you miss me to -

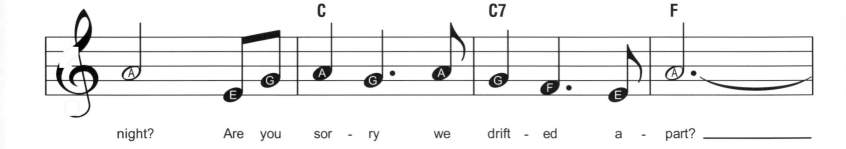

night? Are you sor - ry we drift - ed a - part? _____

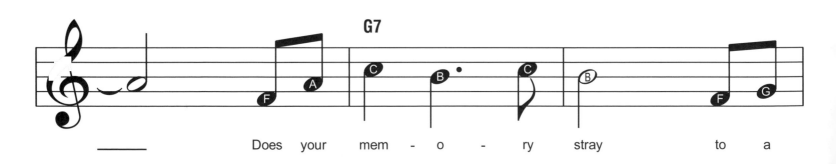

_____ Does your mem - o - ry stray to a

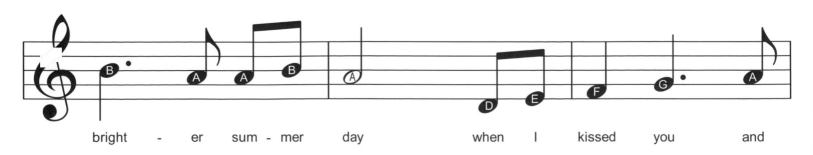

bright - er sum - mer day when I kissed you and

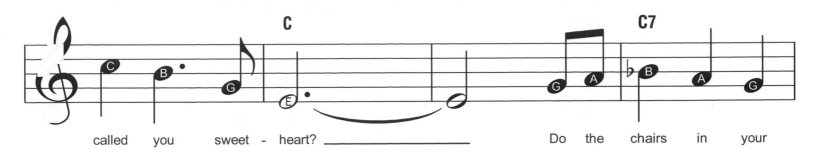

called you sweet - heart? _____ Do the chairs in your

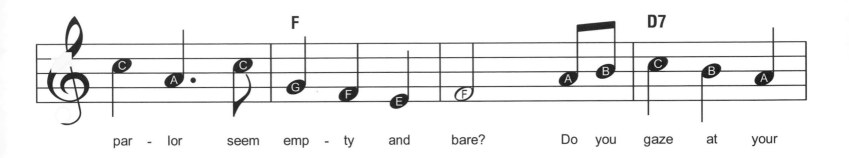

par - lor seem emp - ty and bare? Do you gaze at your

door - step and pic - ture me there? Is your heart filled with

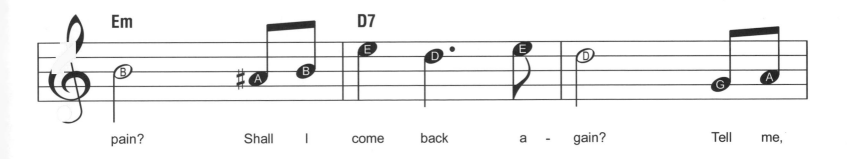

pain? Shall I come back a - gain? Tell me,

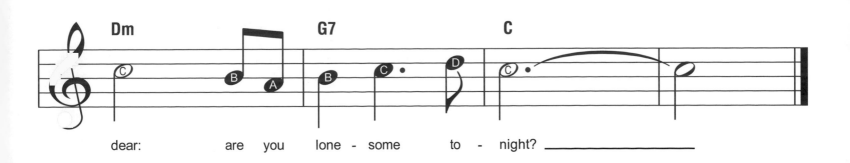

dear: are you lone - some to - night? _____

Blue Suede Shoes

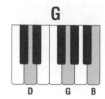
G

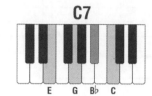
C7

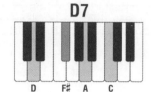
D7

Words and Music by
Carl Lee Perkins

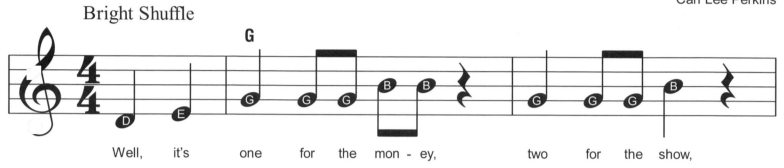

Bright Shuffle

Well, it's one for the mon - ey, two for the show,

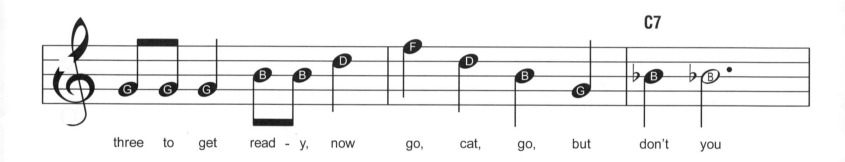

three to get read - y, now go, cat, go, but don't you

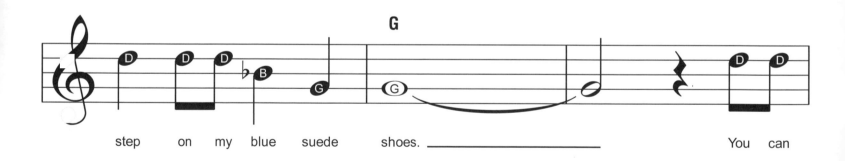

step on my blue suede shoes. _____ You can

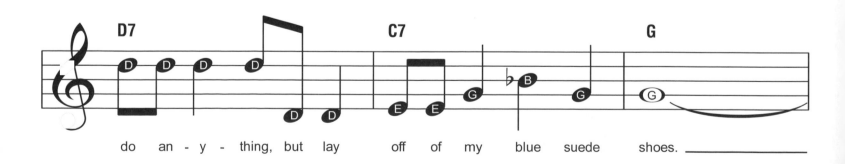

do an - y - thing, but lay off of my blue suede shoes. _____

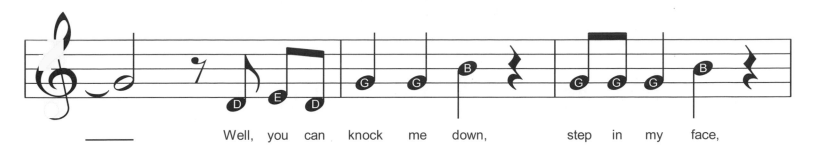

Well, you can knock me down, step in my face,

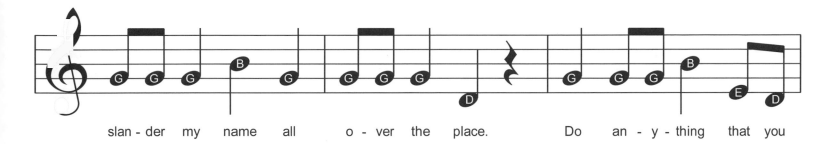

slan - der my name all o - ver the place. Do an - y - thing that you

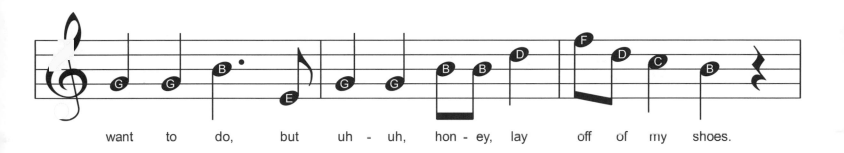

want to do, but uh - uh, hon - ey, lay off of my shoes.

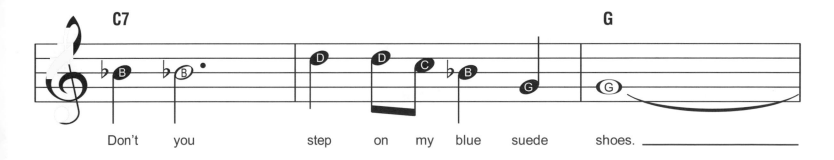

C7   G

Don't you step on my blue suede shoes. _____

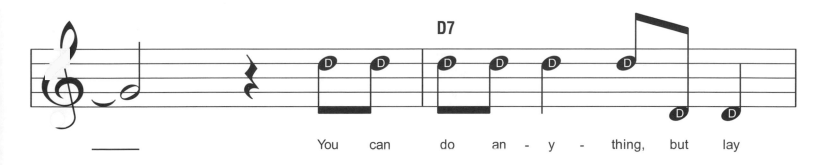

D7

_____ You can do an - y - thing, but lay

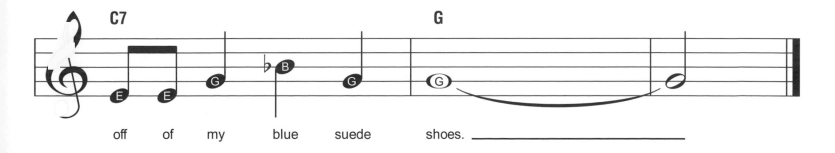

C7   G

off of my blue suede shoes. _____

Burning Love

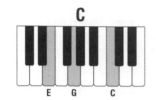
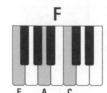
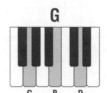
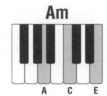

Words and Music by
Dennis Linde

Lord Al - might - y, I feel my tem - p'ra - ture
Ooh, hoo, hoo, _____ I feel my tem - p'ra - ture

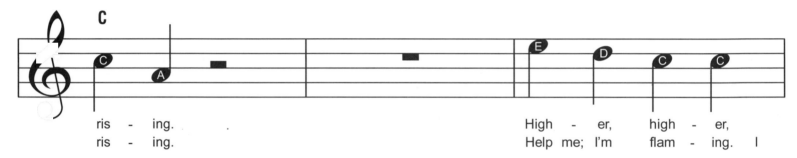

ris - ing. High - er, high - er,
ris - ing. Help me; I'm flam - ing. I

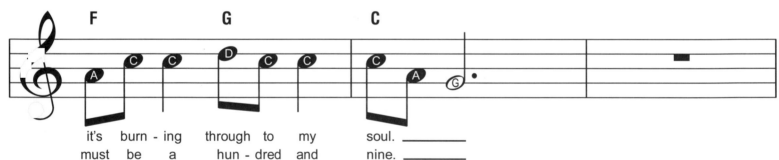

it's burn - ing through to my soul. _____
must be a hun - dred and nine. _____

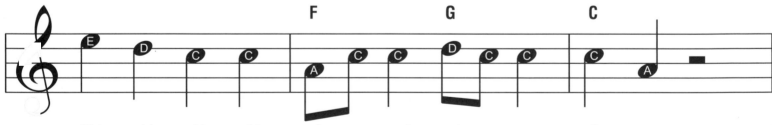

Girl, girl, girl, girl, you've gone and set me on fi - re.
Burn - ing, burn - ing, burn - ing and noth - ing can cool me.

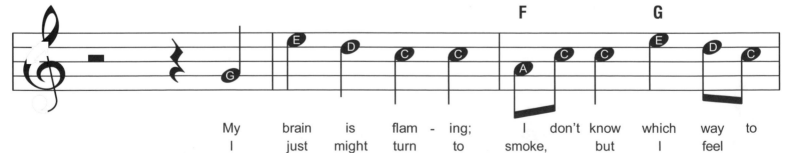

My brain is flam - ing; I don't know which way to
I just might turn to smoke, but I feel

Can't Help Falling in Love

from the Paramount Picture BLUE HAWAII

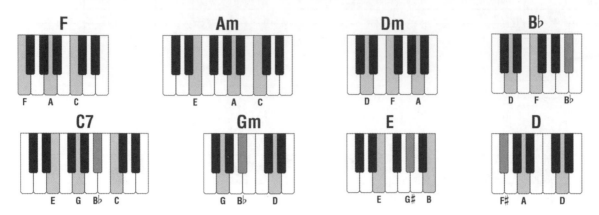

Words and Music by George David Weiss,
Hugo Peretti and Luigi Creatore

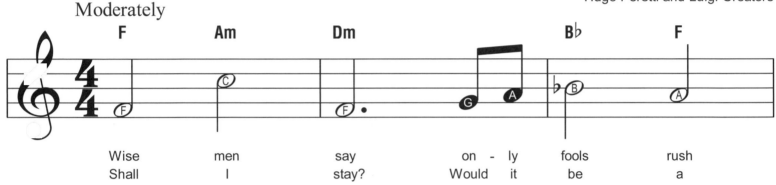

Wise men say only fools rush
Shall I stay? Would it be a

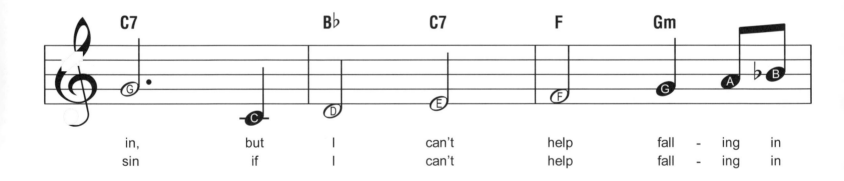

in, but I can't help fall - ing in
sin if I can't help fall - ing in

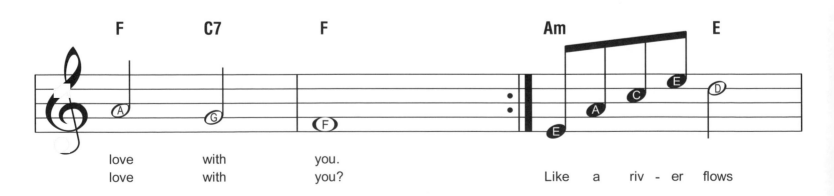

love with you.
love with you? Like a riv - er flows

13

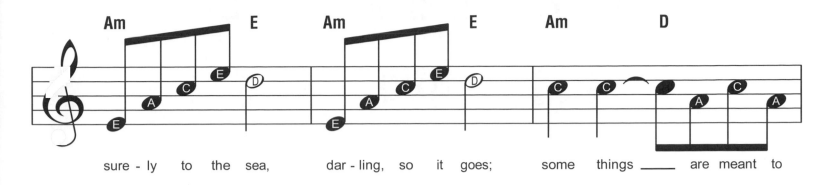

sure - ly   to   the   sea,   dar - ling,   so   it   goes;   some   things _____ are   meant   to

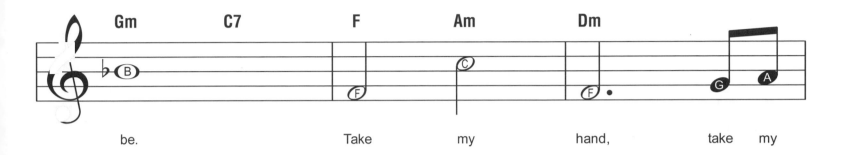

be.   Take   my   hand,   take   my

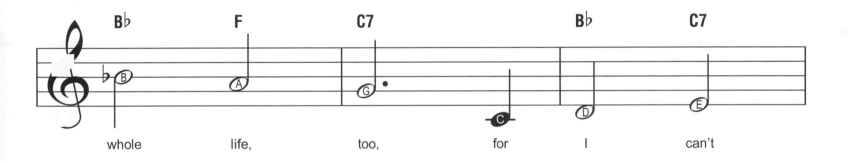

whole   life,   too,   for   I   can't

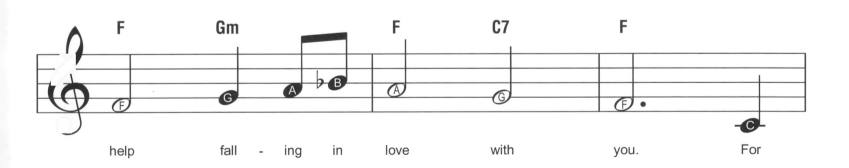

help   fall - ing   in   love   with   you.   For

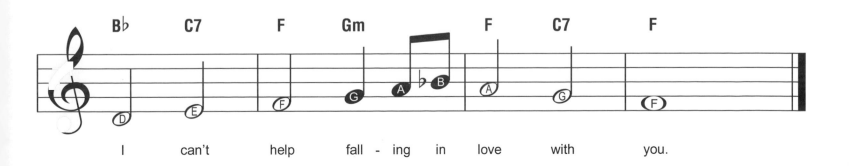

I   can't   help   fall - ing   in   love   with   you.

Cryin' in the Chapel

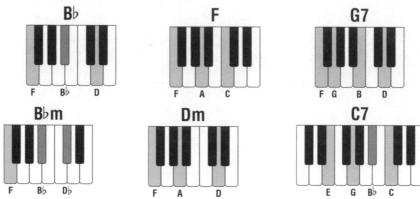

Words and Music by
Artie Glenn

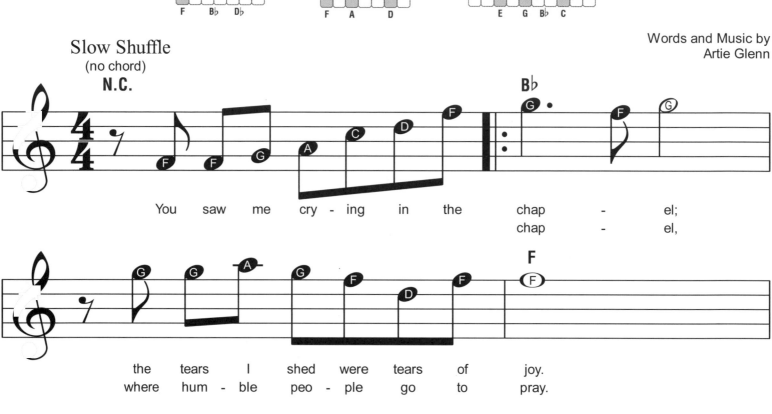

You saw me cry - ing in the chap - el;
chap - el,

the tears I shed were tears of joy.
where hum - ble peo - ple go to pray.

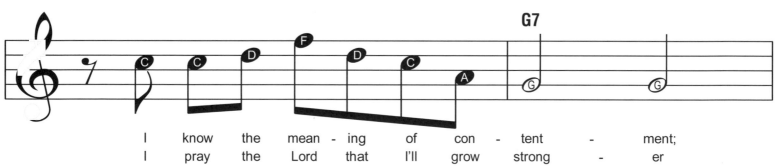

I know the mean - ing of con - tent - ment;
I pray the Lord that I'll grow strong - er

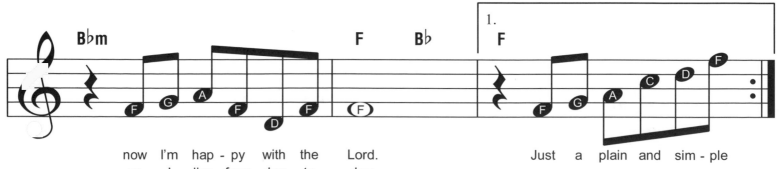

now I'm hap - py with the Lord.
as I live from day to day.

Just a plain and sim - ple

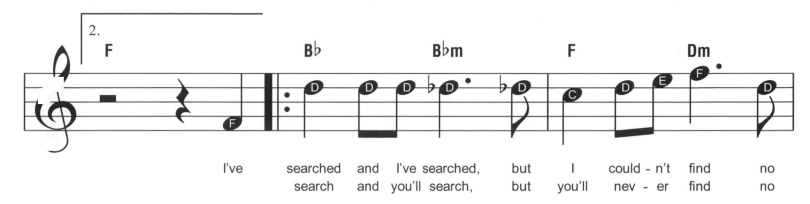

I've   searched   and   I've searched,   but   I   could - n't   find   no
search   and   you'll   search,   but   you'll   nev - er   find   no

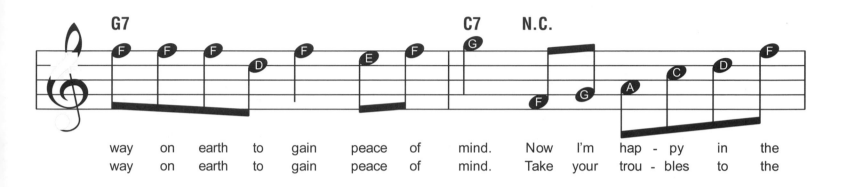

way   on   earth   to   gain   peace   of   mind.   Now   I'm   hap - py   in   the
way   on   earth   to   gain   peace   of   mind.   Take   your   trou - bles   to   the

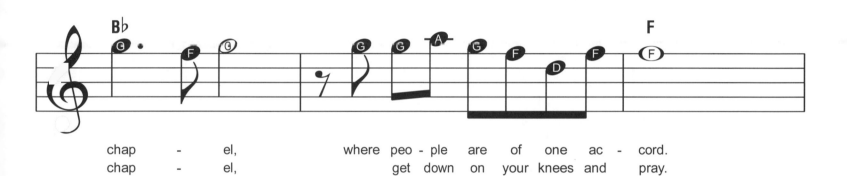

chap - el,   where   peo - ple   are   of   one   ac - cord.
chap - el,   get   down   on   your   knees   and   pray.

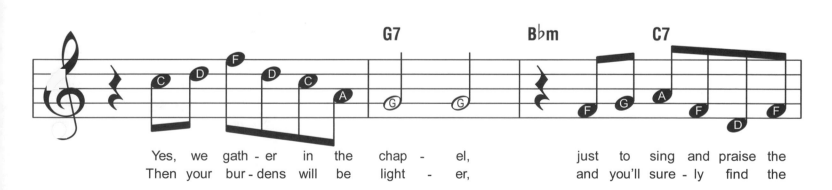

Yes,   we   gath - er   in   the   chap - el,   just   to   sing   and   praise   the
Then   your   bur - dens   will   be   light - er,   and   you'll   sure - ly   find   the

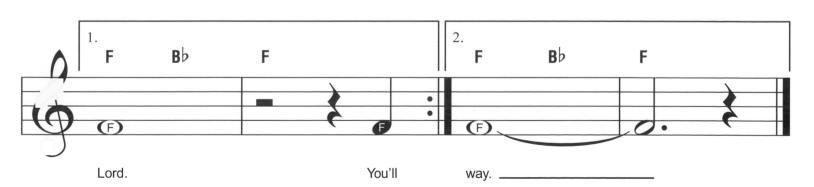

Lord.   You'll   way. _____

(You're The)
Devil in Disguise

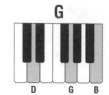
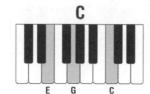
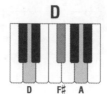
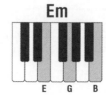

Words and Music by Bill Giant,
Bernie Baum and Florence Kaye

Moderately bright

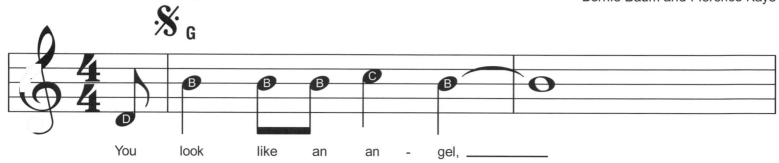

You look like an an - gel, _____

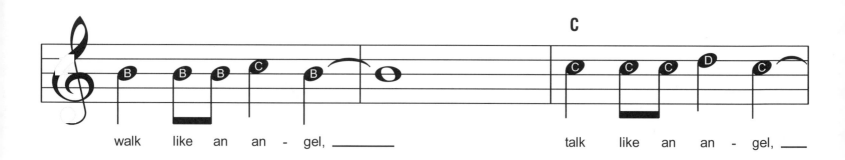

walk like an an - gel, _____   talk like an an - gel, ___

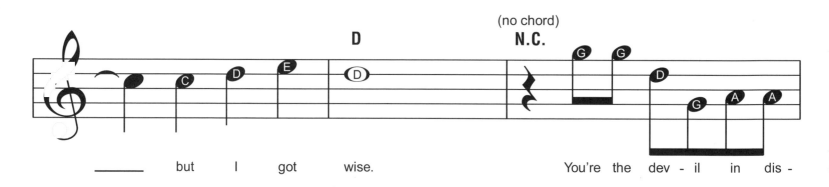

_____ but I got wise.   You're the dev - il in dis -

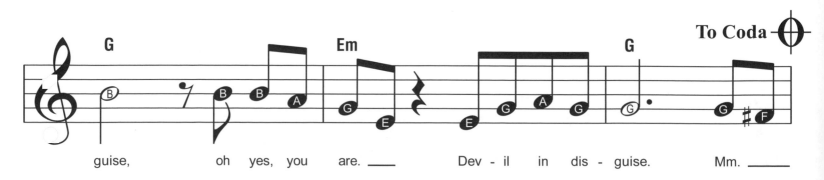

guise, oh yes, you are. ___ Dev - il in dis - guise. Mm. _____

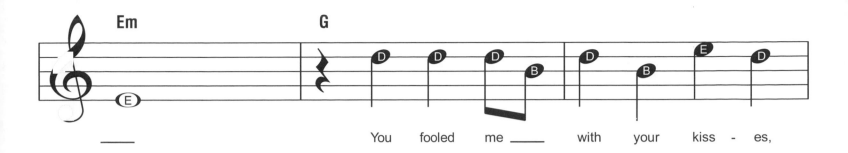

You fooled me ___ with your kiss - es,

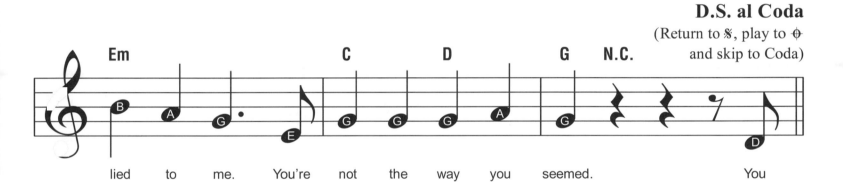

you cheat - ed and you schemed. Heav - en knows how you

D.S. al Coda
(Return to 𝄋, play to ⊕
and skip to Coda)

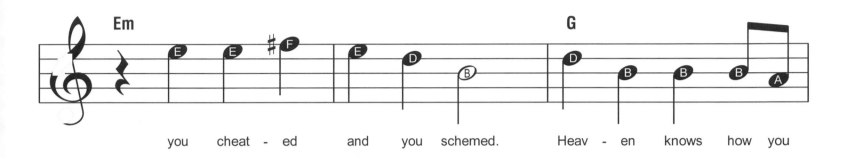

lied to me. You're not the way you seemed. You

CODA

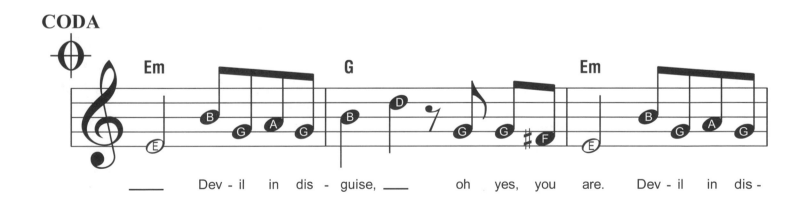

___ Dev - il in dis - guise, ___ oh yes, you are. Dev - il in dis -

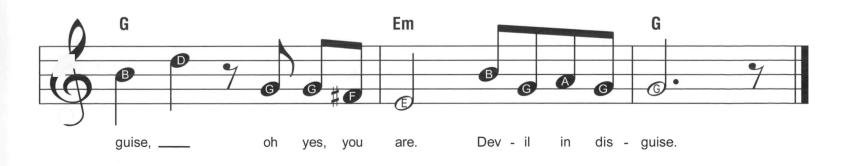

guise, ___ oh yes, you are. Dev - il in dis - guise.

Don't

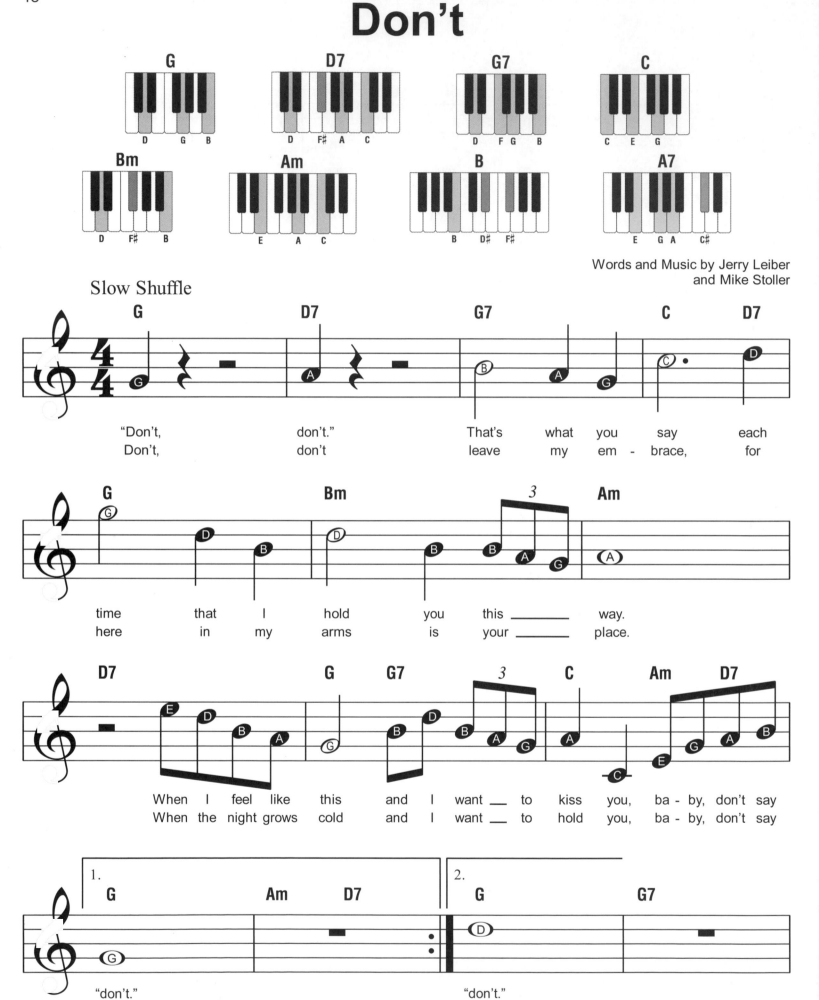

Words and Music by Jerry Leiber
and Mike Stoller

Don't Be Cruel
(To a Heart That's True)

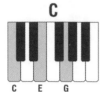
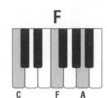
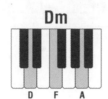
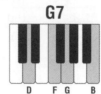

Words and Music by Otis Blackwell
and Elvis Presley

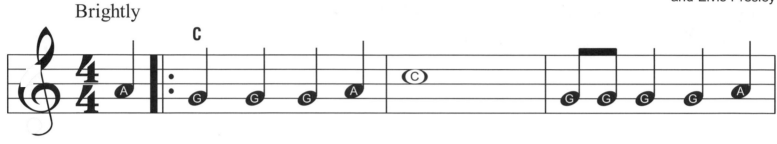

You know I can be found sit - ting home all a -
Ba - by, if I made you mad for some-thing I might have

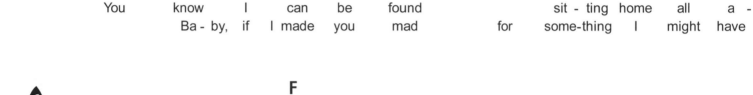

lone. If you can't come a - round, at
said, please, let's for - get my past. The

least, please tel - e - phone. Don't be cruel
fu - ture looks bright a - head. Don't be cruel

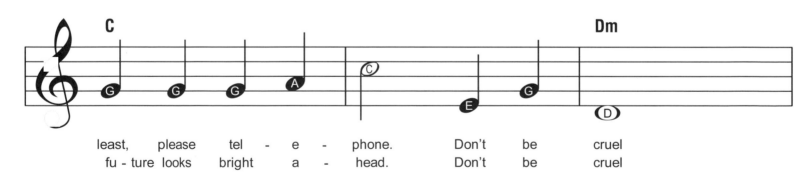

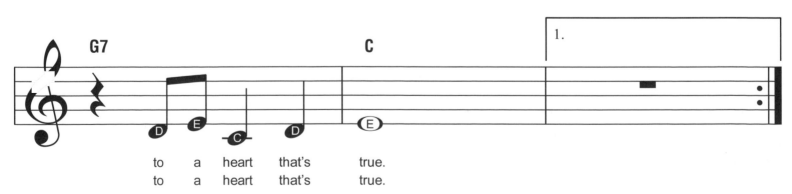

to a heart that's true.
to a heart that's true.

Good Luck Charm

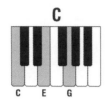
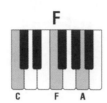
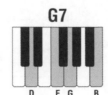
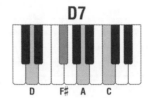

Words and Music by Aaron Schroeder
and Wally Gold

Moderate Shuffle

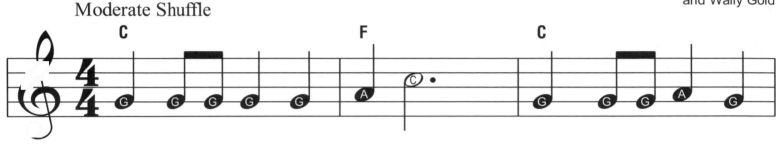

Don't want a four - leaf clo - ver, don't want an old horse -
Don't want a sil - ver dol - lar, rab - bit's foot on a

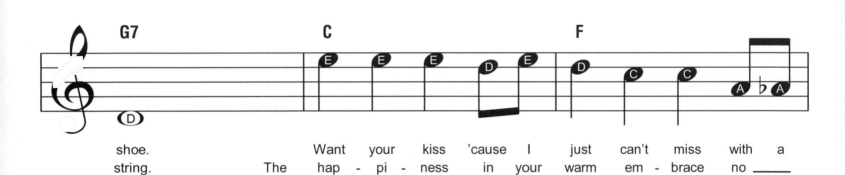

shoe. Want your kiss 'cause I just can't miss with a
string. The hap - pi - ness in your warm em - brace no ____

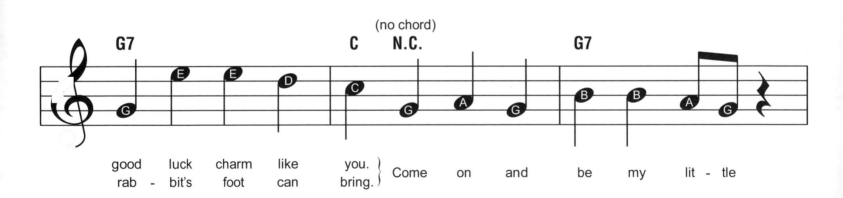

good luck charm like you. } Come on and be my lit - tle
rab - bit's foot can bring.

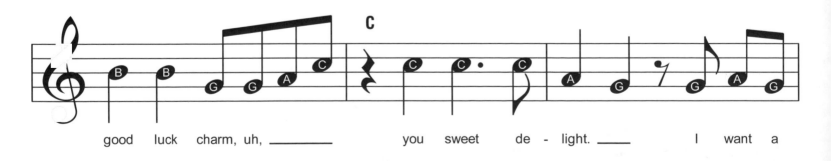

good luck charm, uh, _____ you sweet de - light. ____ I want a

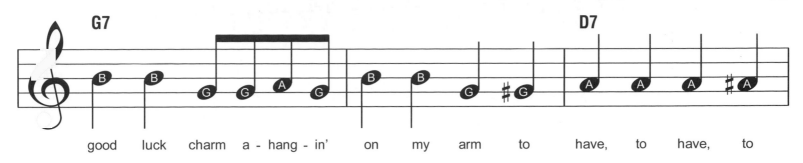

good luck charm a - hang - in' on my arm to have, to have, to

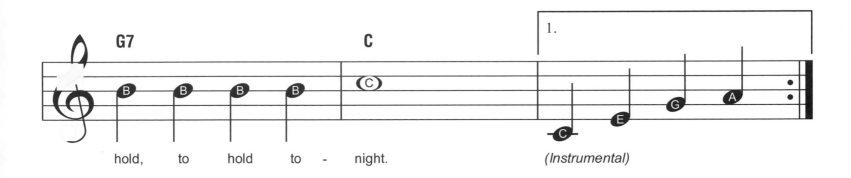

hold, to hold to - night. *(Instrumental)*

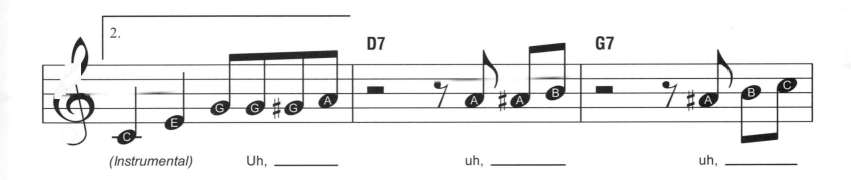

(Instrumental) Uh, _____ uh, _____ uh, _____

oh, yeah. ____ Uh, _____ uh _____

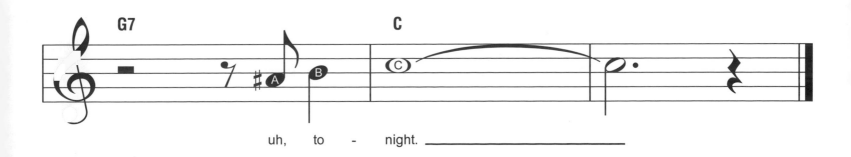

uh, to - night. _____

Hard Headed Woman

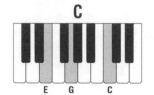
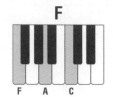
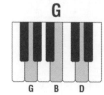

Words and Music by
Claude DeMetruis

Bright Rock

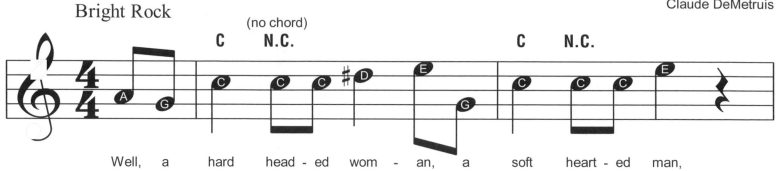

Well, a hard head - ed wom - an, a soft heart - ed man,

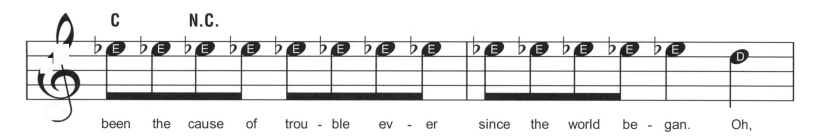

been the cause of trou - ble ev - er since the world be - gan. Oh,

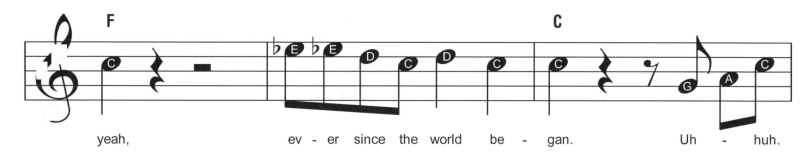

yeah, ev - er since the world be - gan. Uh - huh.

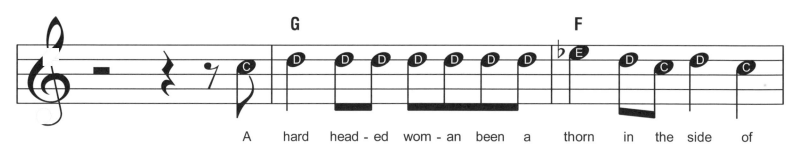

A hard head - ed wom - an been a thorn in the side of

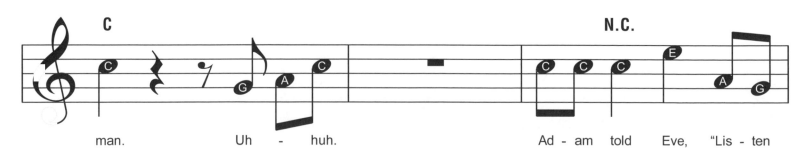

man. Uh - huh. Ad - am told Eve, "Lis - ten

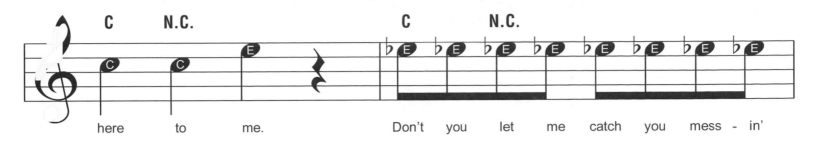

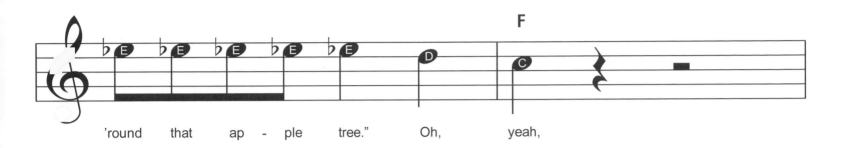

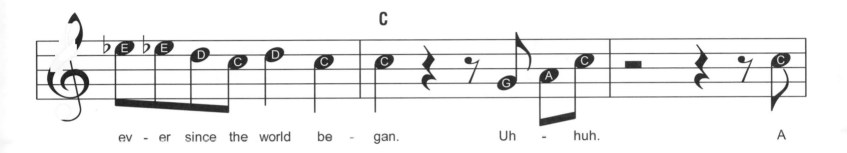

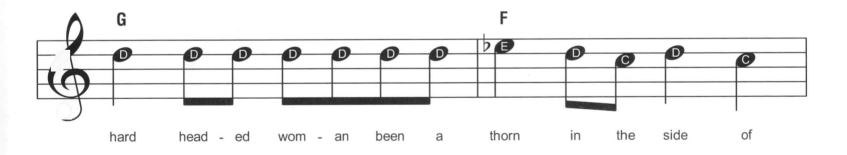

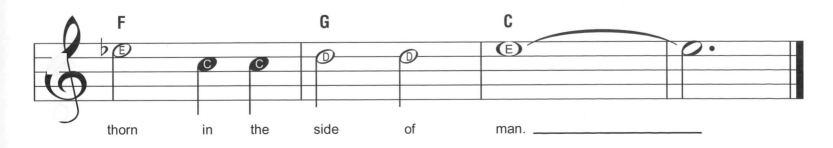

Heartbreak Hotel

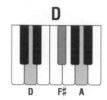
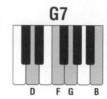
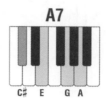

Words and Music by Mae Boren Axton,
Tommy Durden and Elvis Presley

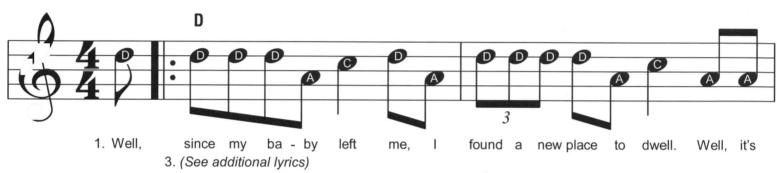

1. Well, since my ba - by left me, I found a new place to dwell. Well, it's
3. *(See additional lyrics)*

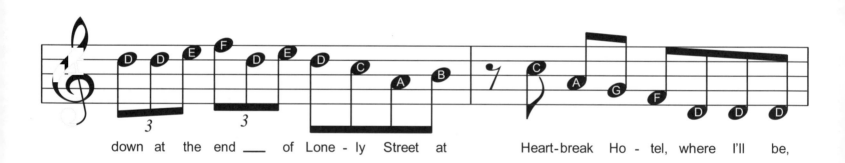

down at the end ___ of Lone - ly Street at Heart - break Ho - tel, where I'll be,

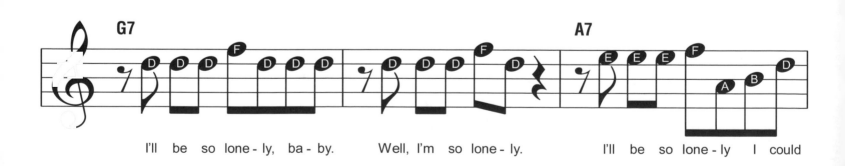

I'll be so lone - ly, ba - by. Well, I'm so lone - ly. I'll be so lone - ly I could

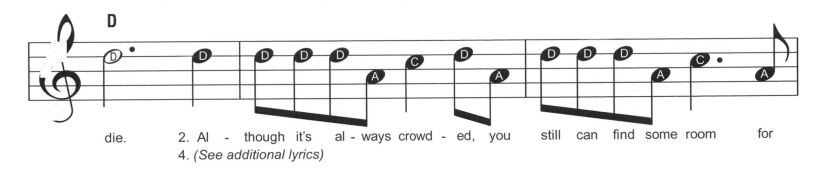

die.   2. Al - though it's al - ways crowd - ed, you still can find some room for
4. *(See additional lyrics)*

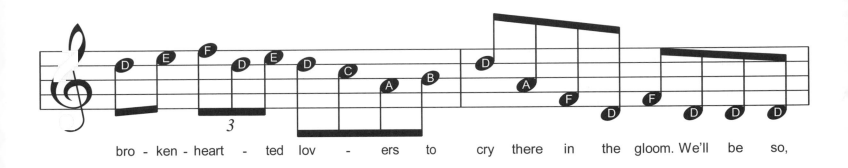

bro - ken - heart - ted lov - ers to cry there in the gloom. We'll be so,

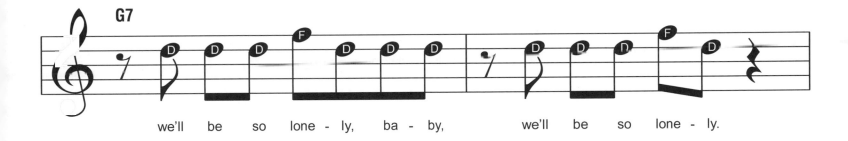

we'll be so lone - ly, ba - by, we'll be so lone - ly.

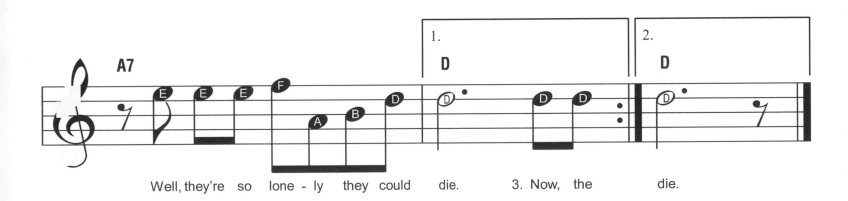

Well, they're so lone - ly they could die.   3. Now, the die.

Additional Lyrics

2. Now, the bellhop's tears keep flowin' and the desk clerk's dressed in black.
   Well, they've been so long on Lonely Street they'll never, never look back, and they're so...
   They'll be so lonely, baby. Well, they're so lonely.
   Well, they're so lonely they could die.

3. Well, now, if your baby leaves you, and you've got a tale to tell,
   Well, just take a walk down Lonely Street to Heartbreak Hotel where you will be...
   You'll be so lonely, baby, where you will be lonely.
   You'll be so lonely you could die.

Hound Dog

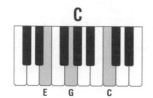
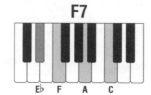

Words and Music by Jerry Leiber
and Mike Stoller

Bright Rock Shuffle

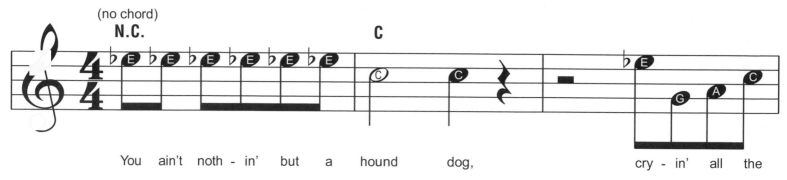

You ain't noth-in' but a hound dog, cry-in' all the

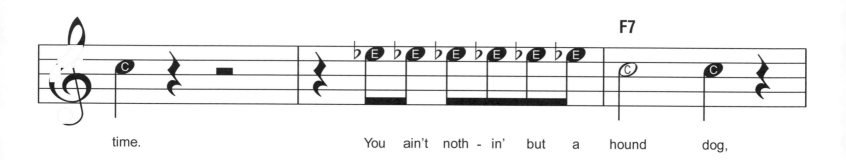

time. You ain't noth-in' but a hound dog,

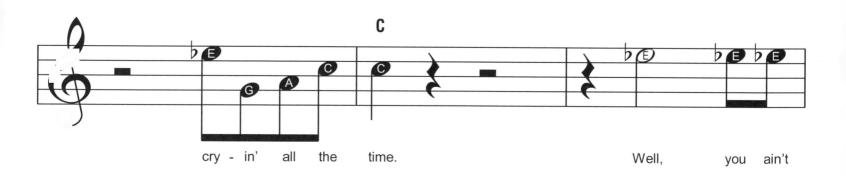

cry - in' all the time. Well, you ain't

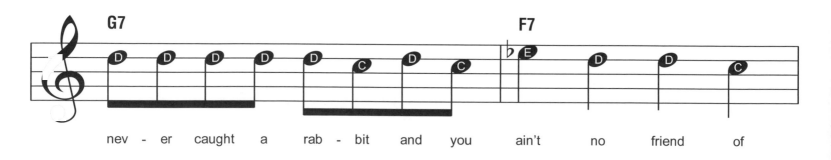

nev - er caught a rab - bit and you ain't no friend of

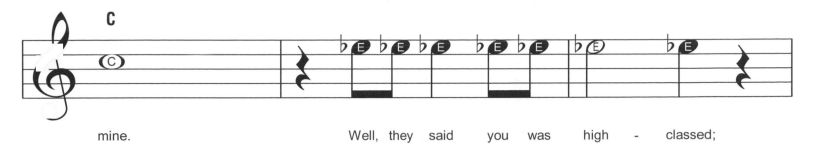

mine.   Well, they said   you   was   high - classed;

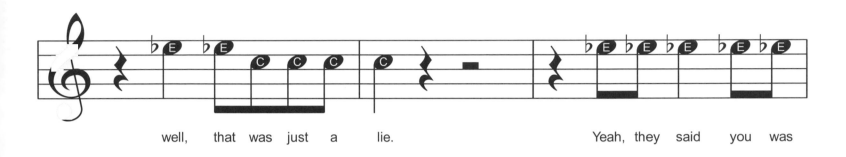

well,   that   was   just   a   lie.   Yeah, they   said   you   was

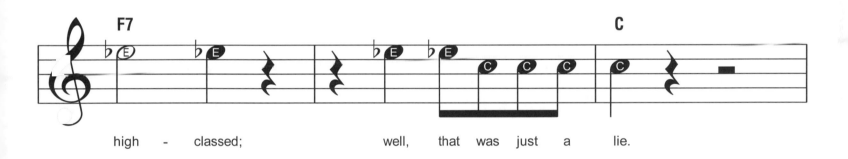

high - classed;   well,   that   was   just   a   lie.

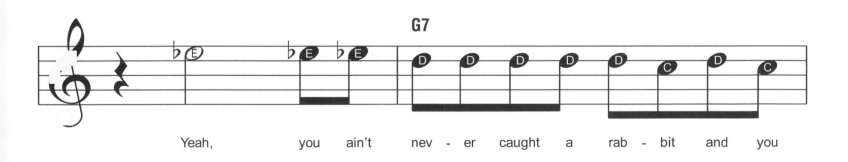

Yeah,   you   ain't   nev - er   caught   a   rab - bit   and   you

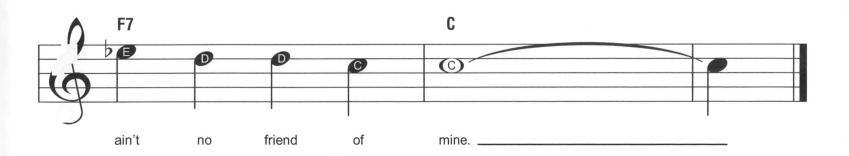

ain't   no   friend   of   mine. _____

It's Now or Never

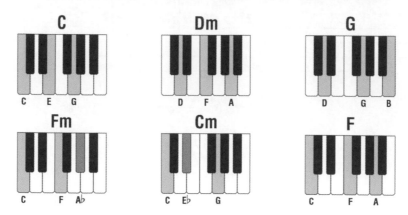

Words and Music by Aaron Schroeder
and Wally Gold

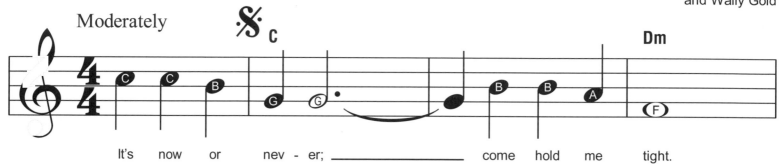

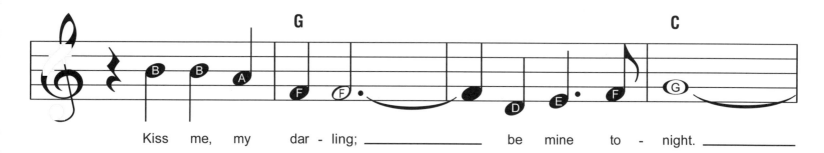

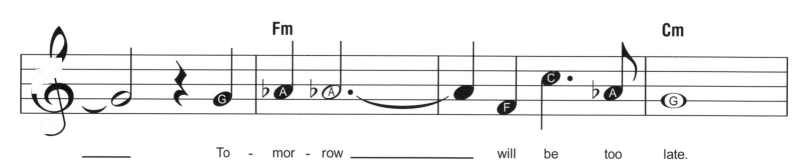

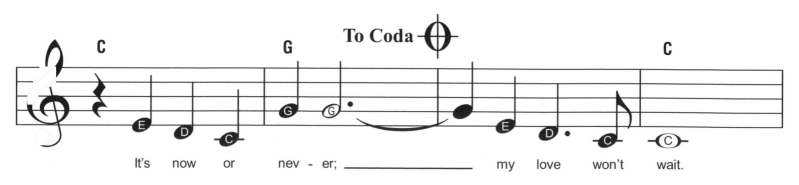

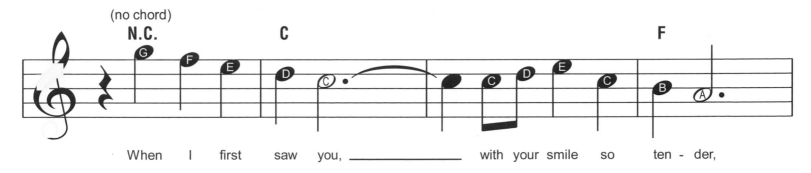

(no chord)
N.C.   C   F

When I first saw you, _____ with your smile so ten-der,

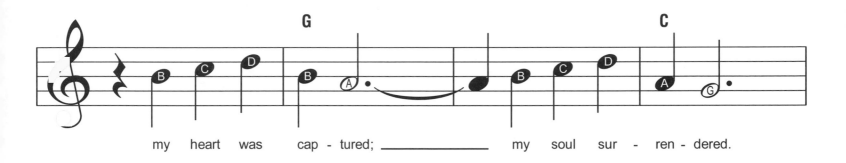

G   C

my heart was cap-tured; _____ my soul sur-ren-dered.

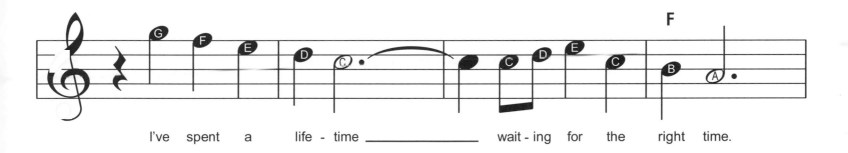

F

I've spent a life-time _____ wait-ing for the right time.

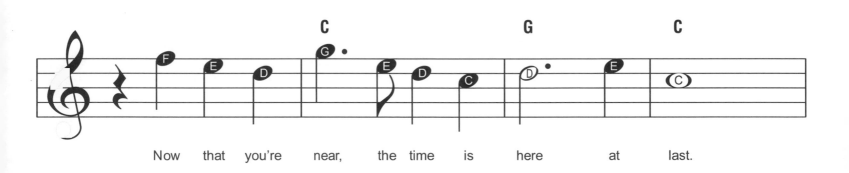

C   G   C

Now that you're near, the time is here at last.

D.S. al Coda
(Return to 𝄉, play to ⊕
and skip to Coda)

CODA

N.C.   C

It's now or _____ my love won't wait. _____

Jailhouse Rock

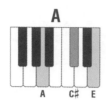
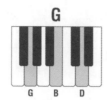
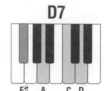
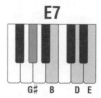

Words and Music by Jerry Leiber
and Mike Stoller

Bright Shuffle

1. The war-den threw a par-ty in the coun-ty jail. The
2.–5. *(See additional lyrics)*

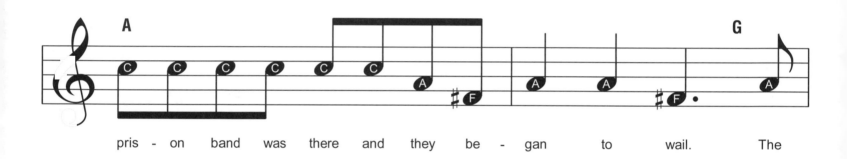

pris-on band was there and they be-gan to wail. The

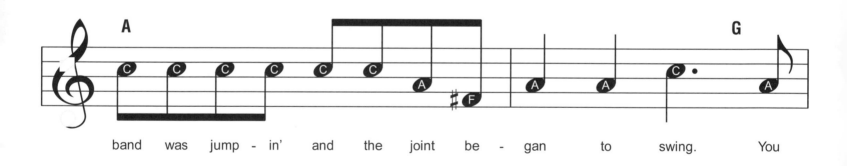

band was jump-in' and the joint be-gan to swing. You

(no chord)

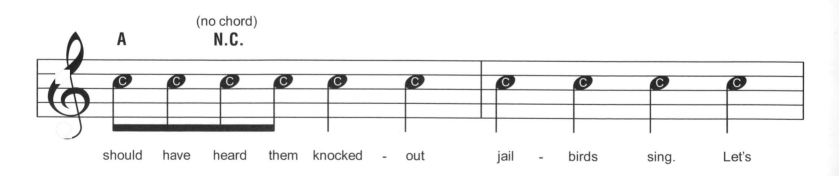

should have heard them knocked-out jail-birds sing. Let's

Chorus

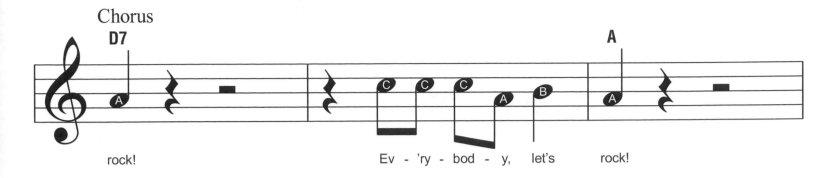

rock!   Ev - 'ry - bod - y,   let's   rock!

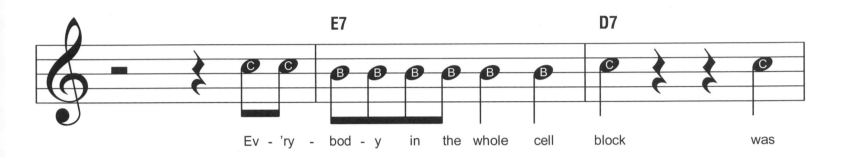

Ev - 'ry - bod - y   in   the   whole   cell   block   was

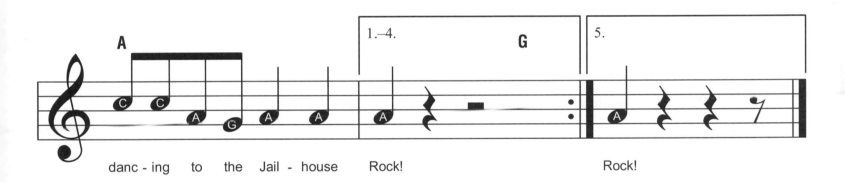

danc - ing   to   the   Jail - house   Rock!   Rock!

Additional Lyrics

2. Spider Murphy played the tenor saxophone,
   Little Joe was blowin' on the slide trombone.
   The drummer boy from Illinois went crash, boom, bang.
   The whole rhythm section was the Purple Gang.
   Chorus

3. Number Forty-seven said to number Three,
   "You're the cutest jailbird I ever did see.
   I sure would be delighted with your company.
   Come on and do the Jailhouse Rock with me."
   Chorus

4. The sad sack was sittin' on a block of stone,
   Way over in the corner weeping all alone.
   The warden said, "Hey, buddy, don't you be no square.
   If you can't find a partner, use a wooden chair!"
   Chorus

5. Shifty Henry said to Bugs, "For heaven's sake,
   No one's lookin'; now's our chance to make a break."
   Bugsy turned to Shifty and he said, "Nix, nix;
   I wanna stick around a while and get my kicks."
   Chorus

Love Me Tender

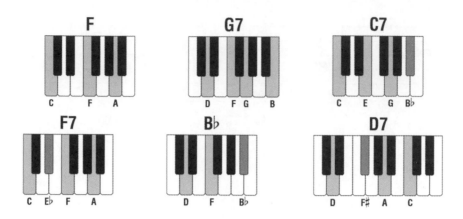

Words and Music by Elvis Presley
and Vera Matson

Moderately slow

Love	me	ten - der,	love	me	sweet;
Love	me	ten - der,	love	me	long;
Love	me	ten - der,	love	me	dear;

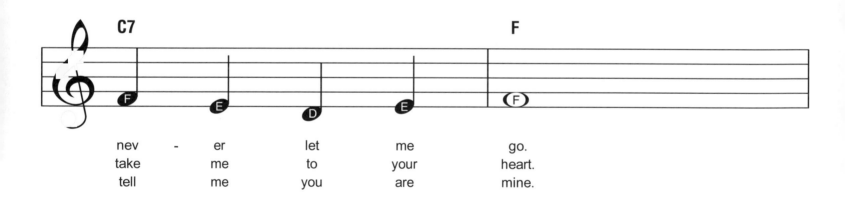

nev - er	let	me	go.
take	me	to	your	heart.
tell	me	you	are	mine.

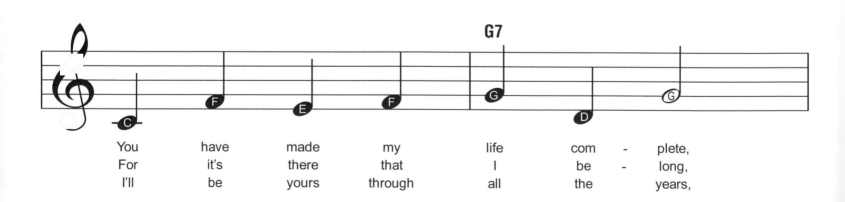

You	have	made	my	life	com - plete,
For	it's	there	that	I	be - long,
I'll	be	yours	through	all	the	years,

Return to Sender
from GIRLS! GIRLS! GIRLS!

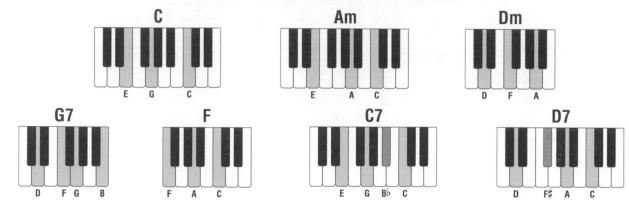

Words and Music by Otis Blackwell
and Winfield Scott

Bright Shuffle

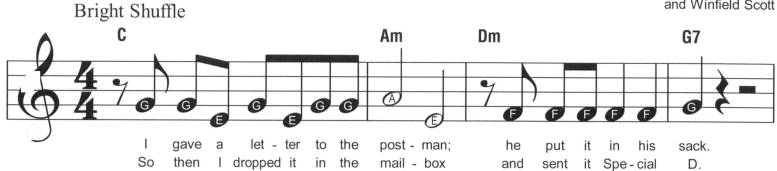

I gave a let-ter to the post-man; he put it in his sack.
So then I dropped it in the mail-box and sent it Spe-cial D.

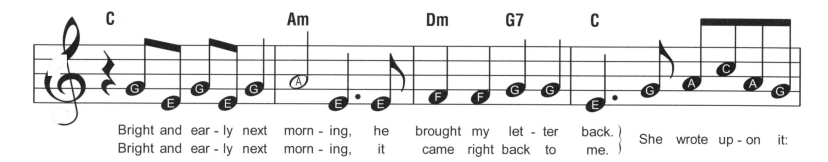

Bright and ear-ly next morn-ing, he brought my let-ter back. }
Bright and ear-ly next morn-ing, it came right back to me. } She wrote up-on it:

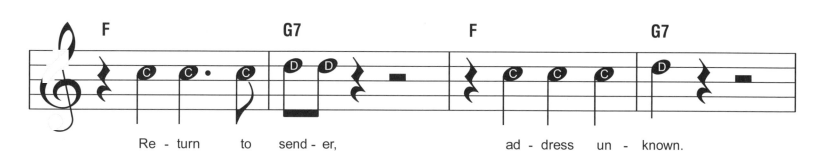

Re - turn to send - er, ad - dress un - known.

To Coda

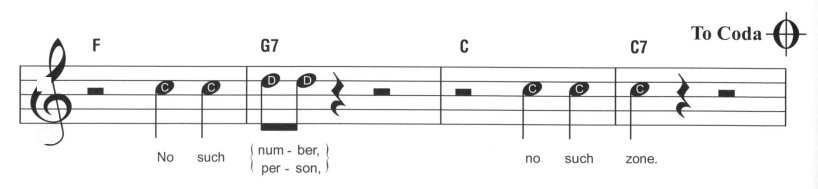

No such { num - ber, / per - son, } no such zone.

We had a quar - rel, a lov - er's spat.

D.C. al Coda
(Return to beginning,
play to ⊕ and skip to Coda)

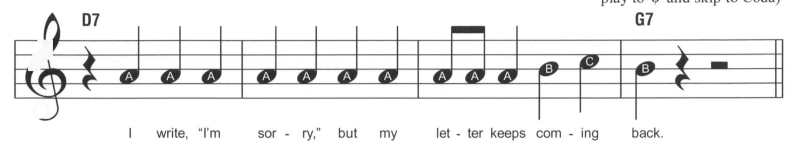

I write, "I'm sor - ry," but my let - ter keeps com - ing back.

CODA

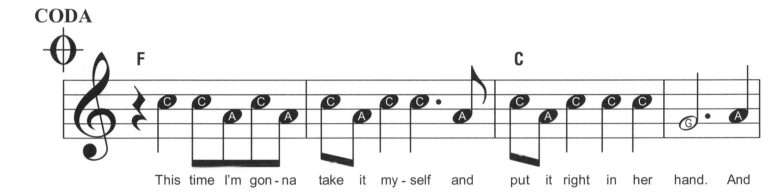

This time I'm gon - na take it my - self and put it right in her hand. And

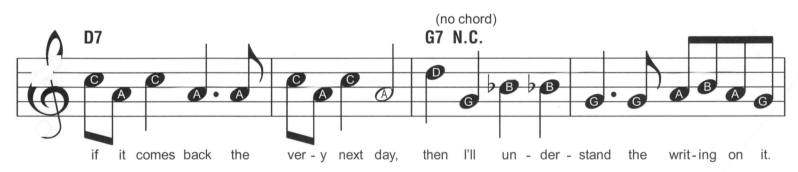

if it comes back the ver - y next day, then I'll un - der - stand the writ - ing on it.

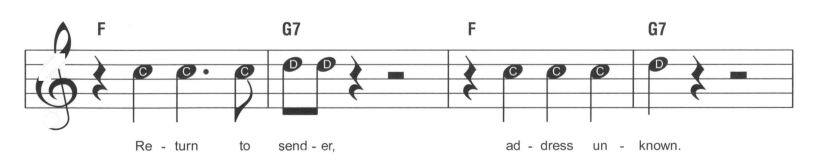

Re - turn to send - er, ad - dress un - known.

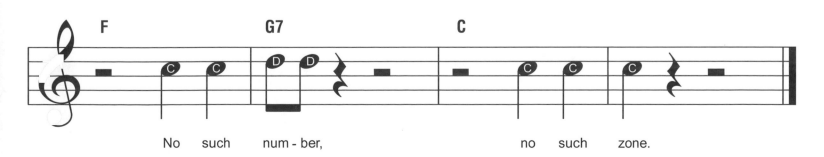

No such num - ber, no such zone.

She's Not You

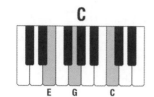
C

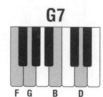
G7

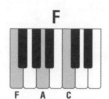
F

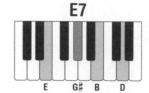
E7

Words and Music by Doc Pomus,
Jerry Leiber and Mike Stoller

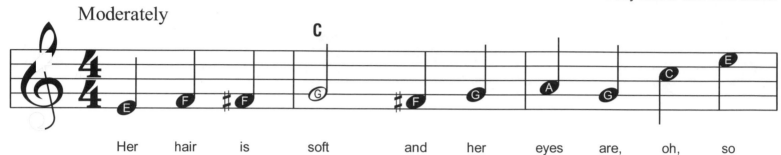

Her hair is soft and her eyes are, oh, so

blue. She's all the things a girl should

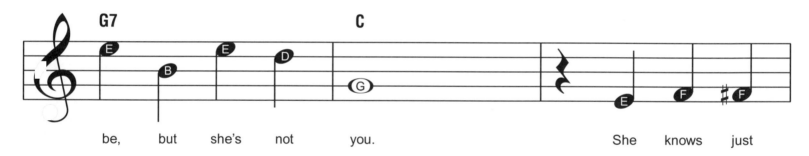

be, but she's not you. She knows just

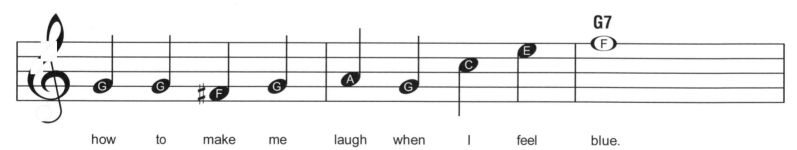

how to make me laugh when I feel blue.

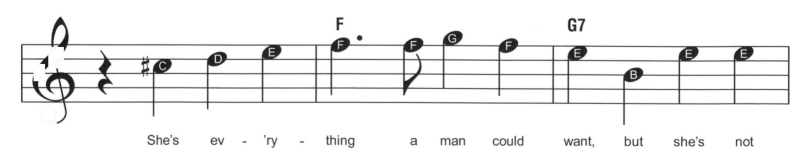

She's ev - 'ry - thing a man could want, but she's not

Suspicious Minds
from ELVIS, THAT'S THE WAY IT IS

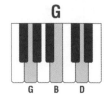
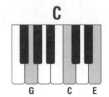
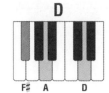
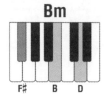

Words and Music by
Francis Zambon

Moderately fast

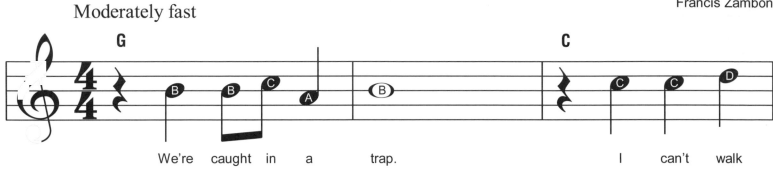

We're caught in a trap. I can't walk

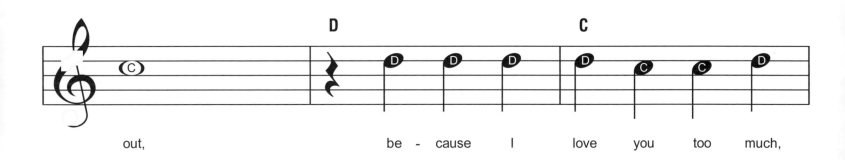

out, be - cause I love you too much,

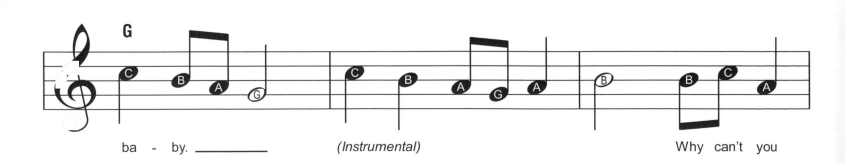

ba - by. _____ (Instrumental) Why can't you

see

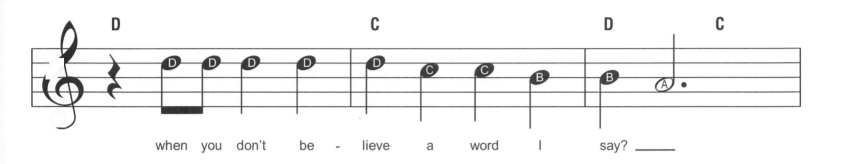

what you're do - ing to me

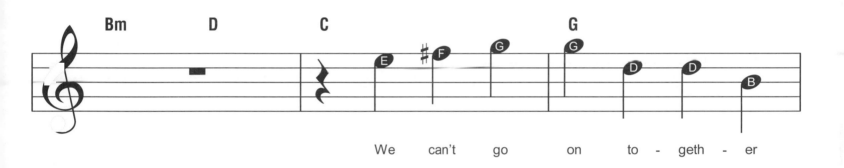

when you don't be - lieve a word I say? _____

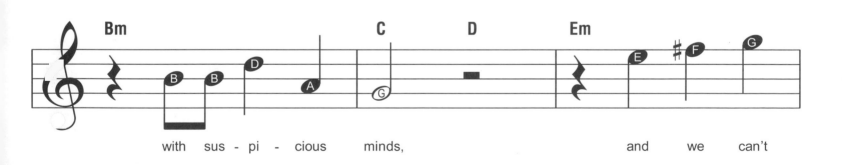

We can't go on to - geth - er

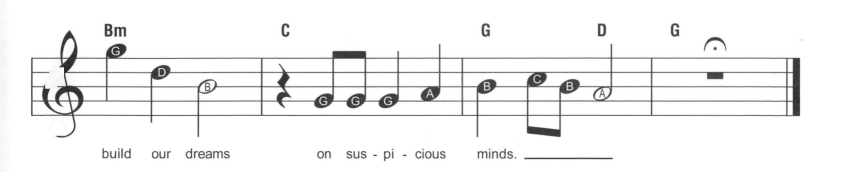

with sus - pi - cious minds, and we can't

build our dreams on sus - pi - cious minds. _____

(Let Me Be Your)
Teddy Bear
from LOVING YOU

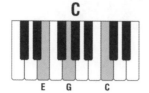
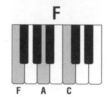
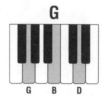

Words and Music by Kal Mann
and Bernie Lowe

Brightly

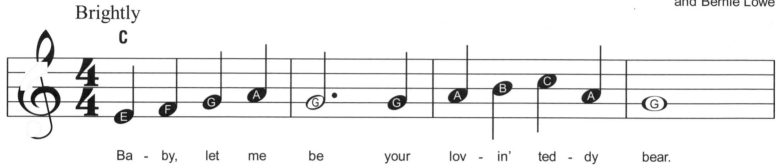

Ba - by, let me be your lov - in' ted - dy bear.

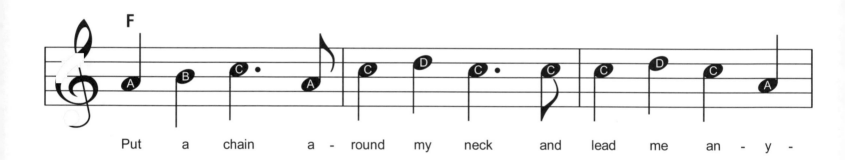

Put a chain a - round my neck and lead me an - y -

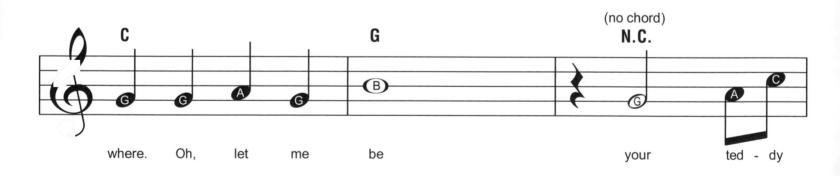

where. Oh, let me be   your ted - dy

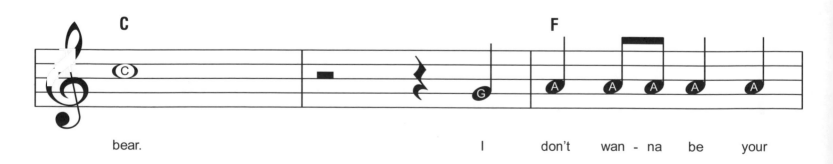

bear.   I don't wan - na be your

Too Much

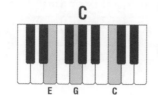

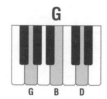
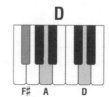

Words and Music by Lee Rosenberg
and Bernard Weinman

Moderate Shuffle

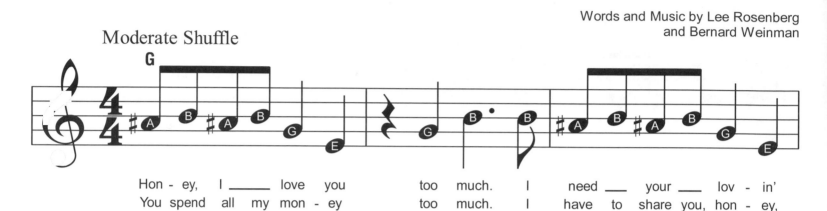

Hon - ey, I ____ love you too much. I need ____ your ____ lov - in'
You spend all my mon - ey too much. I have to share you, hon - ey,

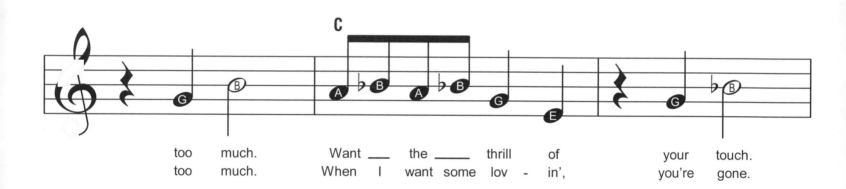

too much. Want ____ the ____ thrill of your touch.
too much. When I want some lov - in', you're gone.

Gee, I can't ____ hold you too much. You do all the liv - in' while
Don't you know you're treat - in' me wrong? Now you got me start - ed; don't you

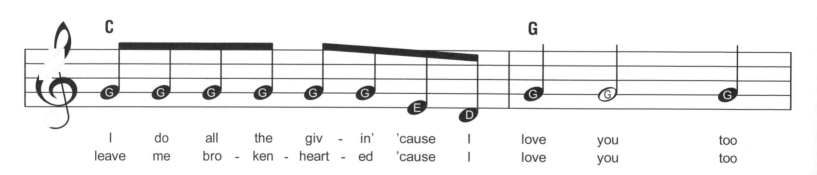

I do all the giv - in' 'cause I love you too
leave me bro - ken - heart - ed 'cause I love you too

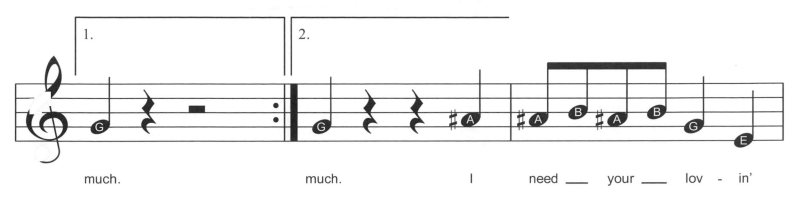

much.　　　　　much.　　　I　need ___ your ___ lov - in'

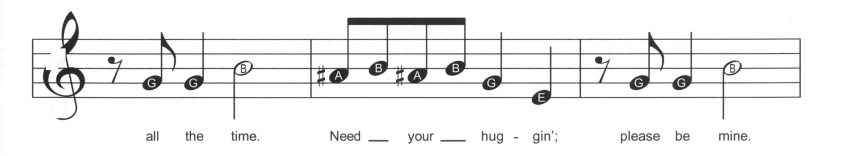

all　the　time.　　Need ___ your ___ hug - gin';　　please　be　mine.

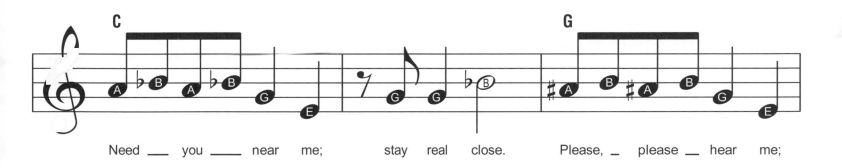

Need ___ you ___ near me;　　stay　real　close.　　Please, _ please _ hear　me;

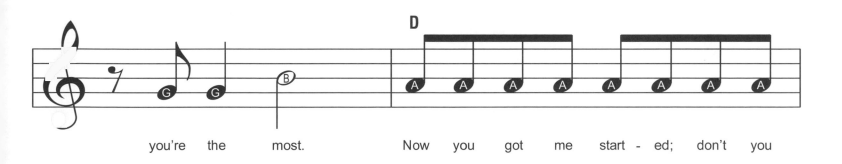

you're　the　most.　　Now　you　got　me　start - ed;　don't　you

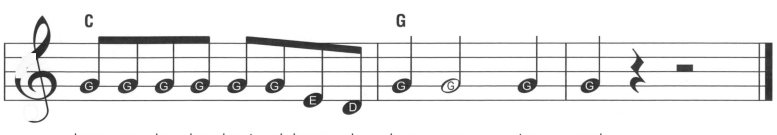

leave　me　bro - ken - heart - ed　'cause　I　love　you　too　much.

Viva Las Vegas

from VIVA LAS VEGAS

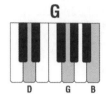
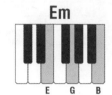
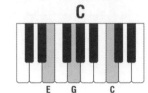
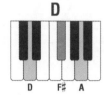

Words and Music by Doc Pomus
and Mort Shuman

Moderately fast

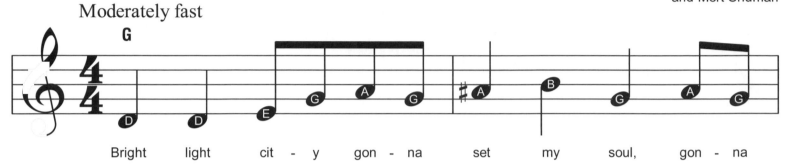

Bright light cit - y gon - na set my soul, gon - na

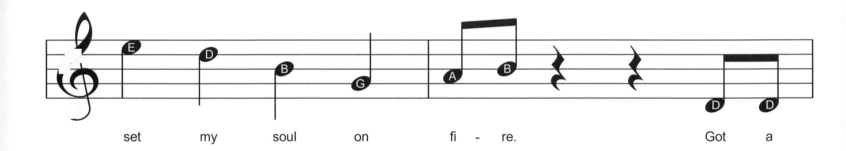

set my soul on fi - re. Got a

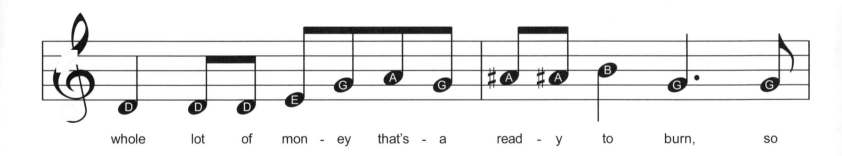

whole lot of mon - ey that's - a read - y to burn, so

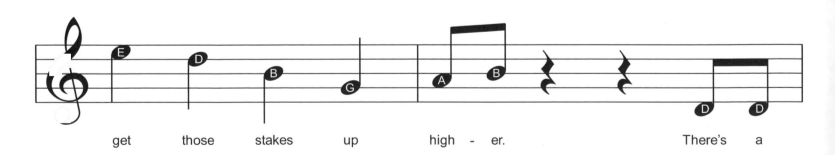

get those stakes up high - er. There's a

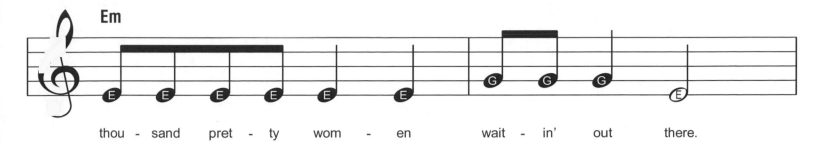

thou - sand pret - ty wom - en wait - in' out there.

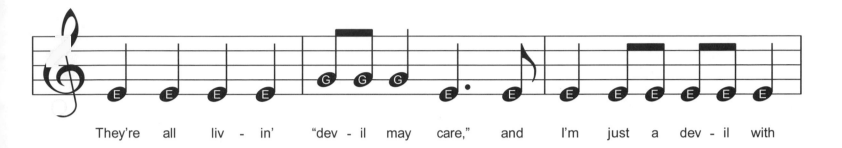

They're all liv - in' "dev - il may care," and I'm just a dev - il with

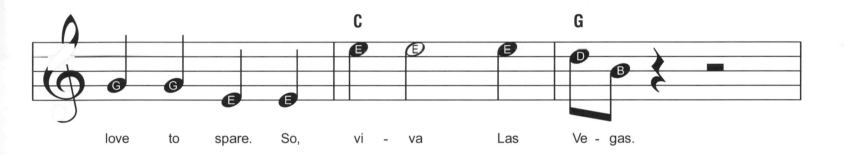

love to spare. So, vi - va Las Ve - gas.

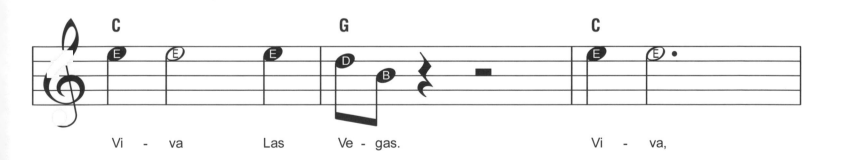

Vi - va Las Ve - gas. Vi - va,

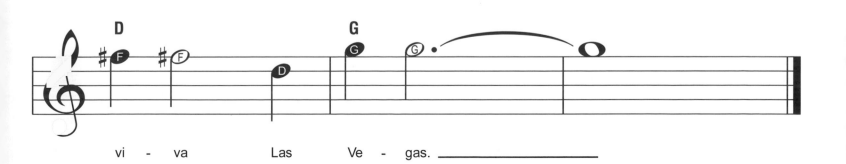

vi - va Las Ve - gas. _____

SUPER EASY SONGBOOK

It's super easy! This series features accessible arrangements for piano, with simple right-hand melody, letter names inside each note, and basic left-hand chord diagrams. Perfect for players of all ages!

THE BEATLES
00198161 60 songs......................$15.99

BEETHOVEN
00345533 21 selections....................$9.99

BEST SONGS EVER
00329877 60 songs......................$15.99

BROADWAY
00193871 60 songs......................$15.99

JOHNNY CASH
00287524 20 songs........................$9.99

CHRISTMAS CAROLS
00277955 60 songs......................$15.99

CHRISTMAS SONGS
00236850 60 songs......................$15.99

CHRISTMAS SONGS WITH 3 CHORDS
00367423 30 songs......................$10.99

CLASSIC ROCK
00287526 60 songs......................$15.99

CLASSICAL
00194693 60 selections................$15.99

COUNTRY
00285257 60 songs......................$14.99

DISNEY
00199558 60 songs......................$15.99

BOB DYLAN
00364487 22 songs......................$12.99

BILLIE EILISH
00346515 22 songs......................$10.99

FOUR CHORD SONGS
00249533 60 songs......................$15.99

FROZEN COLLECTION
00334069 14 songs......................$10.99

GEORGE GERSHWIN
00345536 22 songs........................$9.99

GOSPEL
00285256 60 songs......................$15.99

HIT SONGS
00194367 60 songs......................$15.99

HYMNS
00194659 60 songs......................$15.99

JAZZ STANDARDS
00233687 60 songs......................$14.99

BILLY JOEL
00329996 22 songs......................$10.99

ELTON JOHN
00298762 22 songs......................$10.99

KIDS' SONGS
00198009 60 songs......................$14.99

LEAN ON ME
00350593 22 songs........................$9.99

THE LION KING
00303511 9 songs........................$9.99

ANDREW LLOYD WEBBER
00249580 48 songs......................$19.99

MOVIE SONGS
00233670 60 songs......................$15.99

PEACEFUL MELODIES
00367880 60 songs......................$16.99

POP SONGS FOR KIDS
00346809 60 songs......................$16.99

POP STANDARDS
00233770 60 songs......................$15.99

QUEEN
00294889 20 songs......................$10.99

ED SHEERAN
00287525 20 songs........................$9.99

SIMPLE SONGS
00329906 60 songs......................$15.99

STAR WARS (EPISODES I-IX)
00345560 17 songs......................$10.99

TAYLOR SWIFT
00323195 22 songs......................$10.99

THREE CHORD SONGS
00249664 60 songs......................$15.99

TOP HITS
00300405 22 songs......................$10.99

WORSHIP
00294871 60 songs......................$15.99

Disney characters and artwork TM & © 2021 Disney

HAL•LEONARD®
www.halleonard.com

Prices, contents and availability subject to change without notice.